For John,
Happy Fathers' Day 2002,
With much love & admiration,
♥
Heather

Growing Like a Weed

Other For Better or For Worse® Collections

Love Just Screws Everything Up
Starting from Scratch
"There Goes My Baby!"
Things Are Looking Up . . .
What, Me Pregnant?
If This Is a Lecture, How Long Will It Be?
Pushing 40
It's All Downhill from Here
Keep the Home Fries Burning
The Last Straw
Just One More Hug
"It Must Be Nice to Be Little"
Is This "One of Those Days," Daddy?
I've Got the One-More-Washload-Blues . . .

Retrospectives

Remembering Farley: A Tribute to the Life of Our Favorite Cartoon Dog
It's the Thought That Counts . . . Fifteenth Anniversary Collection
A Look Inside . . . For Better or For Worse: The 10th Anniversary Collection

Growing Like a Weed

by Lynn Johnston

A *For Better or For Worse*® Collection

**Andrews McMeel
Publishing**

Kansas City

ISBN: 0-8362-3685-8

Library of Congress Catalog Card Number: 97-71627

For Better or For Worse® may be viewed on the Internet at
www.unitedmedia.com

— ATTENTION: SCHOOLS AND BUSINESSES —

Andrews McMeel books are available at quantity discounts with bulk purchase for educational, business, or sales promotional use. For information, please write to: Special Sales Department, Andrews McMeel Publishing, 4520 Main Street, Kansas City, Missouri 64111.

13

WELL, THIS IS AN INTERESTING IDEA, BLAIR. WE'D LIKE TO LOOK OVER THESE BROCHURES AND GET BACK TO YOU.

OF COURSE!

EXCEPT THAT THE PRICE WE'RE OFFERING IS ONLY AVAILABLE DURING THIS INTERVIEW! — I'M TELLING YOU, AS A FRIEND, YOU'D BE WISE TO SIGN THESE DOCUMENTS NOW!

NOW?!

YOU'RE ASKING US TO MAKE A $30,000 COMMITMENT WITHOUT THINKING ABOUT IT?!!

OF COURSE NOT!

PLEASE, THINK ABOUT IT!

—YOU HAVE 10 MINUTES.

WHAT DO YOU THINK, EL?

I DON'T KNOW! BUYING A TIME SHARE IS A HUGE COMMITMENT...

...BUT BLAIR IS SO CONVINCING!

SEEMS LIKE A NICE, HONEST GUY, THOUGH—TOLD US ALL ABOUT HIMSELF ....AND IT'S HARD NOT TO TRUST A GUY WHOSE MOTHER'S NAME IS ELLY!!!

WHERE IS HE?

THERE... TALKING TO A LADY BY THE POOL.

PHYLLIS?!! REALLY?!! — MY MOTHER'S NAME IS PHYLLIS!!!

IT'S BEEN NICE TALKING TO YOU, BLAIR, BUT WE'VE DECIDED THAT WE CAN'T AFFORD TO DO THIS RIGHT NOW.

WE APPRECIATE YOUR TIME AND YOUR FRIENDSHIP AND....

ZIP

I DO YOU A FAVOR, AMIGO.....DON'T ASK THOSE PEOPLE IF THEY WANT A FREE LUNCH!

19

DID YOU GET HOME FOR EASTER BREAK MIKE?

YEAH... FOR A COUPLE OF DAYS.

TROUBLE IS, I HAVE SO MUCH WORK TO DO... AN' SO MUCH STUDYING!!

WHY DIDN'T THEY TELL US IT WAS GONNA BE SO HARD? WHY DIDN'T THEY TELL US WE'D BE UP ALL NIGHT - WHY DIDN'T THEY **TELL** US?!!

THEY DID.

... WHY WASN'T I LISTENING?!!

COFFEE! I NEED COFFEE!

WE'RE OUT, MIKE. ZIPPO LEFT.

JODI? KIT?.... OH, MAN - THERE'S FOUR OF US LIVING HERE, AN' NOBODY'S BOUGHT ANY **COFFEE**?!

SORRY!

HOW AM I GONNA STAY **UP** TO STUDY? HOW WILL I STAY **AWAKE** TONIGHT?!

PORK PUFFS

TERROR DOES IT FOR ME.

PORK PUFFS

LOOK, MIKE, THERE'S NO WAY YOU'RE GONNA GET "PERFECT" ON THIS STUFF, OK? SO, STOP BEATING YOURSELF UP!!!

I MEAN, MOST OF THE EXAMS ARE ESSAYS, RIGHT? IT'S NOT LIKE MATH WHERE THE ANSWER IS EITHER RIGHT OR WRONG! ESSAYS ARE EVALUATED BY PEOPLE WHO EITHER LIKE WHAT YOU WRITE, OR THEY DON'T!

IN THIS CASE, WE ARE AT THE MERCY OF THE EDUCATORS. WE ARE AT THE MERCY OF THEIR EGOS, THEIR PREJUDICES, THEIR NARROW-MINDED ADHERENCE TO THE PAST!!!

SO, IF YOU FLUNK THIS EXAM?

... IT'S NOT MY FAULT.

33

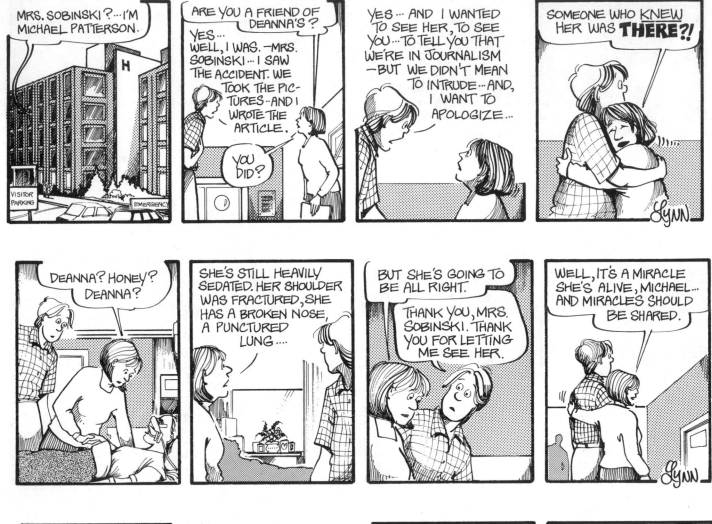

MRS. SOBINSKI?...I'M MICHAEL PATTERSON.

ARE YOU A FRIEND OF DEANNA'S?
YES... WELL, I WAS. —MRS. SOBINSKI...I SAW THE ACCIDENT. WE TOOK THE PICTURES...AND I WROTE THE ARTICLE.
YOU DID?

YES... AND I WANTED TO SEE HER, TO SEE YOU...TO TELL YOU THAT WE'RE IN JOURNALISM —BUT WE DIDN'T MEAN TO INTRUDE...AND, I WANT TO APOLOGIZE...

SOMEONE WHO KNEW HER WAS **THERE**?!

DEANNA? HONEY? DEANNA?

SHE'S STILL HEAVILY SEDATED. HER SHOULDER WAS FRACTURED, SHE HAS A BROKEN NOSE, A PUNCTURED LUNG....

BUT SHE'S GOING TO BE ALL RIGHT.
THANK YOU, MRS. SOBINSKI. THANK YOU FOR LETTING ME SEE HER.

WELL, IT'S A MIRACLE SHE'S ALIVE, MICHAEL... AND MIRACLES SHOULD BE SHARED.

WELL, WE GOT A PHOTO AN' SOME OF YOUR COPY ONTO THE FRONT PAGE, MIKE. —ISN'T THAT WHAT WE'VE BEEN STUDYING FOR?
I GUESS...

THAT WON'T BE THE LAST ACCIDENT WE'LL COVER, MAN. IF WE'RE GONNA BE JOURNALISTS, THERE'LL BE OTHER SERIOUS THINGS WE'LL HAVE TO WRITE ABOUT!
I KNOW.

BUT, NEXT TIME, IT'LL BE DIFFERENT, WEED.
YEAH. —NEXT TIME, WE'LL HAVE SOME EXPERIENCE!

...NEXT TIME, WE'LL HAVE SOME COMPASSION.

HELLO, MICHAEL.

HELLO, RHETTA. — YOU WANTED TO SPEAK TO ME?

HOW CAN I BEGIN?... LOOK, I KNOW IT WAS ME WHO WANTED TO BREAK UP AT CHRISTMAS... BUT I NEVER STOPPED CARING ABOUT YOU!

MICHAEL, COULD WE GET BACK TOGETHER AGAIN? I KNOW I HURT YOU ... BUT I'M A DIFFERENT PERSON NOW! THINGS HAVE CHANGED!

LIKE, THE GUY YOU DUMPED ME FOR, HAS DUMPED YOU?

WELL... YEAH.

Lynn

RHETTA, I DON'T THINK I'M READY TO START ALL OVER AGAIN.

I UNDERSTAND. REALLY.

MICHAEL, DATING SOMEONE ELSE WAS GOOD FOR ME. IT GAVE ME A CHANCE TO SEE HOW GOOD OUR RELATIONSHIP WAS! ... AND WHAT IT WAS LIKE WITHOUT YOU.

NOW, I KNOW THAT IT'S YOU I WANT TO BE WITH! — BUT I UNDERSTAND HOW YOU FEEL. YOU NEED TO THINK IT OVER ... AND MAYBE, IN TIME, WE CAN PICK UP THE PIECES!

I DON'T KNOW, RHETTA.

— YOU CAN PICK UP ALL THE GLASS, ... BUT YOU CAN'T REMAKE THE WINDOW.

Lynn

YOU'RE AWFULLY QUIET TONIGHT. IS SOMETHING ON YOUR MIND?

NO. WELL... MAYBE.

MOM, RHETTA WANTS US TO GET TOGETHER AGAIN — AND THAT WOULD HAVE BEEN GREAT, EXCEPT THAT I'VE JUST MET SOMEONE ELSE WHO IS WONDERFUL AND I WANT TO SEE WHERE IT GOES!!

SHOULD I GO BACK WITH RHETTA? SHOULD I CALL DEANNA? WHAT SHOULD I DO?

WELL, I THINK THE DECISION IS YOURS, HONEY. YOU SHOULD GO WHEREVER YOUR HEART LEADS YOU.

Lynn

SO, MICHAEL AND RHETTA ARE TOGETHER AGAIN, ARE THEY. I WONDERED HOW THAT WOULD TURN OUT.

I DON'T THINK I'D WANT TO START DATING AGAIN, CONNIE... GOING THROUGH ALL OF THE UNCERTAINTY ...NOT KNOWING IF YOU WERE IN LOVE OR IN NEED.

YEAH. I LIKE THE CONSISTENCY OF MARRIAGE. I LIKE THE CHALLENGE. I LIKE KNOWING THAT SOMEONE IS THERE FOR ME, EVERY DAY, THROUGH THICK AND THIN.

LATELY, I'D SAY... IT'S BEEN MOSTLY "THICK".

KNOW WHAT, EL? I JUST FIGURED OUT THAT YOU AND I HAVE KNOWN EACH OTHER FOR 30 YEARS !!

REALLY?

WHO WOULD HAVE GUESSED THAT WE'D STILL BE FRIENDS AFTER ALL THIS TIME! — FROM MINI-DRESS TO MENOPAUSE!

DON'T SAY THAT WORD, CONNIE.

I LIKE TO THINK OF IT AS "A PERIOD OF ADJUSTMENT."

I LIKE TO THINK OF IT AS "NO PERIOD AT ALL !!"

WHAT'S THE MATTER, EL?

I'M TOO HOT.

I CAN'T SLEEP. I FEEL BLOATED AND DEPRESSED AND IRRITABLE.

I WISH I COULD SLEEP LIKE YOU CAN! YOU JUST LIE DOWN, SHUT YOUR EYES AND PASS OUT !!

MEN DON'T HAVE TO LIVE WITH ALL THE PHYSICAL INCONVENIENCES WOMEN HAVE TO LIVE WITH!

TRUE...

— WE JUST HAVE TO LIVE WITH THE WOMEN.

55

WHAT'S HAPPENING, LIZ?

MOM ASKED LAWRENCE TO CHECK OUT THE GARDEN. YOU SHOULD HEAR HIM TALK ABOUT SOIL, MIKE. THE STUFF HE KNOWS IS AMAZING!

THIS WILL HELP TO NEUTRALIZE THE ACIDITY HERE, AND I'VE BROUGHT YOU A NEW PEAT AND LOAM MIXTURE TO TRY OUT.

WHERE'S YOUR MOTHER, MIKE?

OUT BACK, TALKING TO THE NEIGHBORS...

AN' GETTING SOME OF THE LATEST DIRT.

62

IF YOU AN' BRIAN TOOK OVER THE GAS STATION FOR 48 HOURS, AN' BEN AND I TOOK OVER FOR 48, THAT'D GIVE GORDO AN' TRACEY A LONG WEEKEND OFF!

WE COULD WORK IT OUT, MAN! — WE COULD DO IT!!

YEAH! — I GUESS WE COULD!

WE NEVER GAVE THEM MUCH WHEN THEY GOT MARRIED... THIS COULD BE A BELATED WEDDING GIFT!

AN' WHEN YOU THINK ABOUT IT — THIS IS THE BEST KIND OF GIFT YOU COULD GIVE!

YEAH!

...IT'S FREE!

HEY, MOM, LAWRENCE AN' I GOT IT ALL WORKED OUT SO TRACE AN' GORDO CAN TAKE SOME TIME OFF!

THAT'S GREAT, HONEY!

BUT, YOU DON'T KNOW ANYTHING ABOUT RUNNING A GAS STATION, MIKE!

WHAT'S TO KNOW?

BESIDES, IT'S GOOD RESEARCH. —AS A WRITER, I NEED TO EXPERIENCE DIFFICULTY... AND, IF I GET INTO TROUBLE, I'LL DO WHAT ANY SENSIBLE AND MATURE PERSON WOULD DO.

...HE'LL CALL DAD.

YOUR NEW SHRUBS ARE ALL IN, MRS. P. I'LL BE BACK TO CHECK ON THEM AGAIN TOMORROW.

THANKS, LAWRENCE!

OH, AND I PUT A NEW WIRE FENCE AROUND YOUR FLOWER BEDS....TO KEEP THE "VARMINTS" OUT!

DON'T WORRY! — WE'LL SHOO AWAY THE CATS, CAPTURE THE RODENTS, AND WE'LL KEEP THE DOG WELL AWAY FROM THE GARDEN.

MOM?

...HE MEANS ME.

63

65

Panel 1: "DAD, COULD I ASK YOU A PERSONAL QUESTION?" "SURE, MIKE. WHAT IS IT?"

Panel 2: "DID YOU REALLY INVEST IN GORDON'S BUSINESS?" "YES, WE DID. — I GUESS YOU COULD CALL US 'PARTNERS'."

Panel 3: "WHAT IF SOMETHING HAPPENS? WHAT IF YOU DON'T GET YOUR MONEY BACK?" "THAT'S A POSSIBILITY ALL RIGHT!"

Panel 4: "... BUT I LIKE TO TAKE A GAMBLE NOW AND THEN. — AND I'D NEVER BET ON A HORSE THAT I DIDN'T THINK WOULD WIN!!"

Panel 5: "WASN'T THAT A NICE EVENING, KIDS? I THINK IT WAS A LOVELY EVENING!"

Panel 6: "AND THE BEST PART WAS THAT WE WERE ALL TOGETHER! WASN'T IT NICE BEING ALL TOGETHER?"

Panel 7: "MOM, MICHAEL NEVER STOPPED BUGGING ME, APRIL GOT DIRT ALL OVER HERSELF, AN' I WAS, LIKE TOTALLY BORED!!!"

Panel 8: "SIGH... JUST LIKE OLD TIMES!"

Panel 9: "SO GORDON AND TRACEY ARE GOING TO TAKE A HOLIDAY!" "UH-HUH... AS SOON AS THEY CAN!"

Panel 10: "IT WAS A NICE IDEA THAT LAWRENCE HAD, CONNIE." "AND IT WAS NICE OF MICHAEL TO GO ALONG WITH IT!"

Panel 11: "WE'VE GOT GOOD KIDS, EL. THEY'RE THOUGHTFUL AND CONSIDERATE — AND THERE ISN'T A THING THEY WOULDN'T DO FOR OTHER PEOPLE!" "YEAH..."

Panel 12: "... WON'T IT BE GREAT WHEN THEY START DOING STUFF FOR US!!!"

66

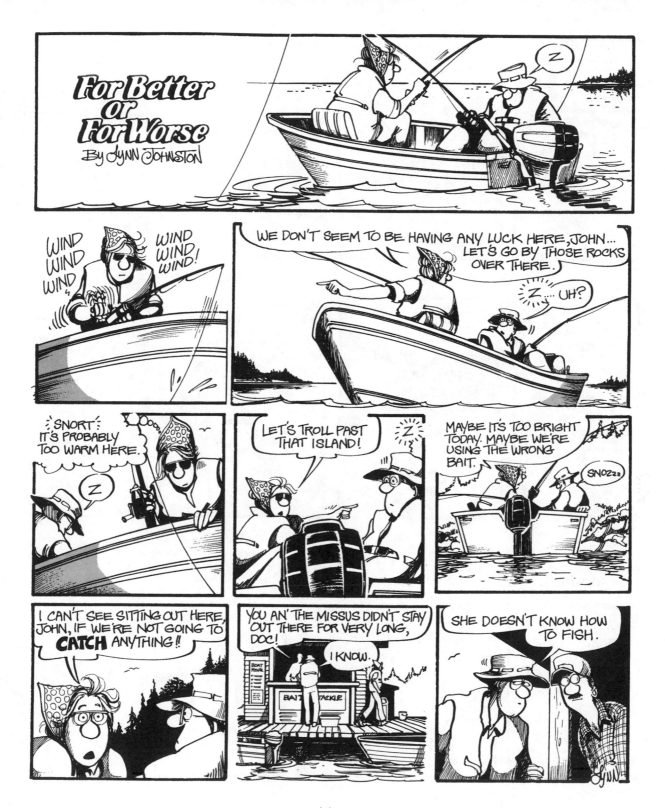

WELL, LIZ—I SEE COUSIN LAURA TOOK YOU OUT ON THE HORSES!

IT MUST HAVE BEEN A LONG RIDE!

HOW DID YOU KNOW?

LOOK AT YOU!

... LAST TIME I SAW A BODY WALK LIKE THAT, WAS AFTER HERB SNELGROOT HAD HIS VASECTOMY!!

WE'VE FINISHED OUR CHORES, DAD! COULD YOU DRIVE US INTO TOWN? PLEEEASE?

WHAT'S GOIN' ON IN TOWN THAT YOU'RE ALL STEAMED UP ABOUT?

THERE'S ANOTHER FIRE DOWN AT RUNCIE'S CHIP STAND, AN' THEY CAN'T PUT IT OUT, 'CAUSE BOOGER HARRIS BACKED HIS FRONT-END LOADER INTO THE FIRE TRUCK!!

IN THIS NECK OF THE WOODS, WE TEND TO CREATE OUR OWN ENTERTAINMENT.

THIS SURE IS A SMALL TOWN, LAURA.

WHEN I WENT INTO THE BANK, THE TELLER KNEW MY NAME, WHERE I WAS FROM, AN' HOW LONG I WAS STAYING!

THIS SURE WOULD BE A WEIRD PLACE TO LIVE IF YOU NEEDED PRIVACY!

YEAH...

BUT, IT'S ONE OF THE BEST PLACES ON EARTH IF YOU NEEDED HELP.

84

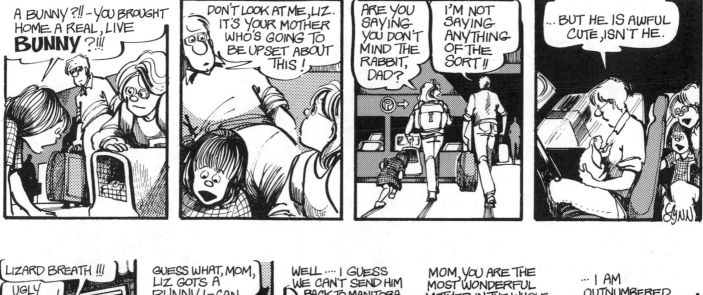

87

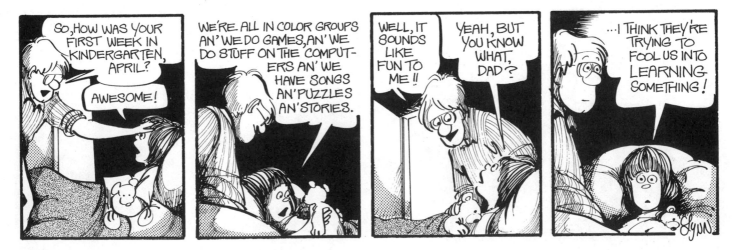

WANNA COME OVER TO MY PLACE AFTER SCHOOL, DAWN?

SURE!

IS IT OK IF SHAWNA-MARIE COMES ALONG? SHE AN' I, LIKE, GOT TOGETHER WHILE YOU WERE OUT OF TOWN.

SHE IS SO COOL, LIZ! SHE'S TEACHING ME HOW TO MEDITATE AN' HER BROTHER HAS A REAL STOCK CAR—AN' HE RACES IT, TOO!!

WE HAD SUCH AN AWESOME TIME THIS SUMMER!

REALLY!

... I SHOULD GO AWAY MORE OFTEN!

Lynn

SO SHAWNA-MARIE AN' I ENDED UP WORKING TOGETHER AT THE ICE CREAM CIRCUS! —YOU KNOW, WITH THE CLOWN HATS AN' STUFF?

FOR THE WHOLE MONTH OF AUGUST, WE WORKED THE HARD ICE CREAM COUNTER, DIGGING OUT CONES DAY AFTER DAY...

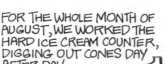

'TIL WE COULDN'T STAND IT!!

DID YOU GET PAID?

HEY, WE MORE THAN GOT PAID, APRIL!

... WE GOT PIPES!

Lynn

SO, WE'RE TAKING OFF, LIZ!

I'M GONNA SHOW DAWN SOME YOGA... AN' THEN WE'RE GONNA DO OUR MANTRAS.

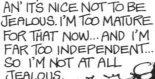

I'M NOT JEALOUS. DAWN'S BEST FRIENDS NOW WITH SHAWNA-MARIE, BUT I'M NOT JEALOUS.

AN' IT'S NICE NOT TO BE JEALOUS. I'M TOO MATURE FOR THAT NOW... AND I'M FAR TOO INDEPENDENT... SO I'M NOT AT ALL JEALOUS.

I'M ALONE, I'M TOTALLY BUMMED... BUT I'M NOT JEALOUS.

Lynn

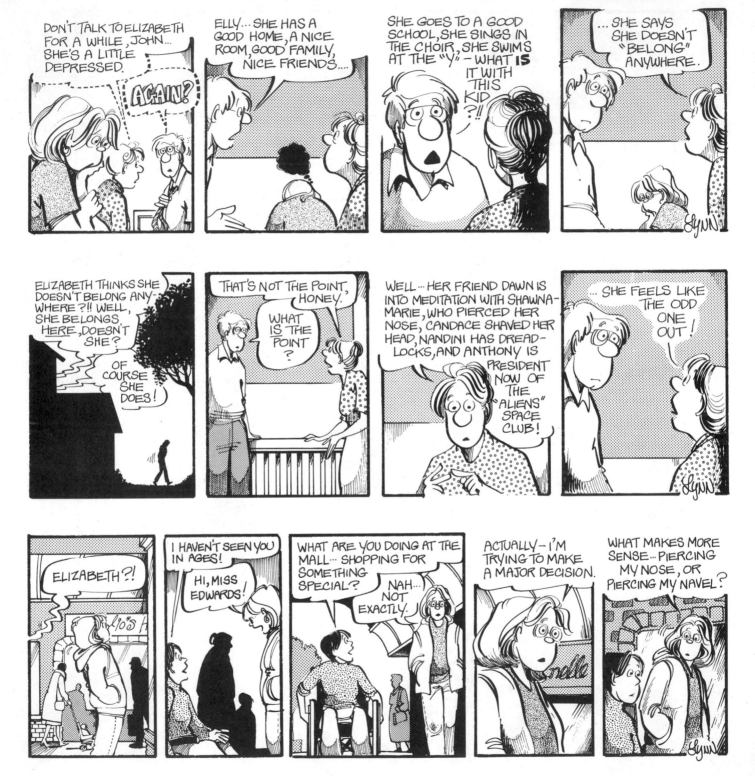

MUNCH!

BUT DADDY
HE ONLY SITS
ON YOUR LAP
IF HE REALLY
LIKES
YOU !!!

Panel 1: ELIZABETH, YOUR RABBIT IS CHEWING HOLES IN THINGS AGAIN!

Panel 2: I'VE TOLD YOU BEFORE — DON'T LET HIM OUT IF YOU'RE NOT GOING TO WATCH WHAT HE'S DOING!!

Panel 3: I NEVER LET HIM OUT OF HIS CAGE... **APRIL** DID!!

Panel 4: I DUNNO, EL... I'D SAY SHE'S PASSING THE "BUCK"!

Panel 5: ELIZABETH, WHEN YOU BROUGHT THE RABBIT HOME, I TOLD YOU I WASN'T GOING TO BE THE ONE WHO LOOKS AFTER HIM!

Panel 6: HE'S YOUR RABBIT, SO HE'S YOUR RESPONSIBILITY, UNDERSTAND?

Panel 7: SO FIND A WAY TO KEEP HIM CLEAN AND CARED FOR, OR HE'LL HAVE TO GO!!
OK.

Panel 8: APRIL... HOW WOULD YOU LIKE TO OWN MY RABBIT?

Panel 9: YOU REALLY MEAN IT? YOU'RE REALLY GONNA GIVE YOUR BUNNY TO ME?
UH HUH. HE'S ALL YOURS.

Panel 10: OH, WOW! DID YOU HEAR THAT, MR. B? YOU BELONG TO ME NOW!!

Panel 11: THAT MEANS YOU HAFTA FEED HIM AN' CLEAN HIS CAGE FROM NOW ON.
I WILL!

Panel 12: BUT I CAN STILL PLAY WITH HIM WHENEVER I WANT TO.
OK!

Panel 13: THANKS, 'LIZABETH!
HEY... I JUST WANTED TO DO YOU A FAVOR.

110

Panel 1: HELLO, RABBIT. I BROUGHT YOU SOME CARROT PEELINGS.

Panel 2: OK. YOU CAN COME OUT FOR A WHILE.

Panel 3: YOU ARE AWFULLY CUTE.

Panel 4: ....BUT DON'T EXPECT OURS TO BE A PERSONAL RELATIONSHIP. ....DON'T EXPECT ME TO BECOME ATTACHED TO YOU.

Lynn

Panel 1: MOM, DO YOU LIKE THE BUNNY NOW? — SURE. I LIKE THE BUNNY!

Panel 2: ARE YOU GLAD WE GOTS A DOG AN' A BUNNY? — YES, APRIL. I THINK PETS ARE GOOD TO HAVE. THEY'RE AN IMPORTANT PART OF GROWING UP!

Panel 3: DO YOU REALLY, REALLY, REALLY LIKE THEM? — YES... I REALLY DO! — WHY?

Panel 4: 'CAUSE I BROUGHT HOME **ANOTHER** ONE !!!

Lynn

Panel 1: HERE WE ARE AT THE BUNG AND WATTLE... STUDENT OASIS, WALK-IN CLINIC AND HOME AWAY FROM HOME!

Panel 2: MAN, IT'S BUSY IN HERE TONIGHT. — FIRST-YEAR KIDS, MOSTLY. — YEAH — THE "PARTY 'TIL YOU DROP OUT" CROWD.

Panel 3: IN SECOND YEAR, YOU TAKE YOUR EDUCATION MORE SERIOUSLY. — RIGHT... STUDY FIRST, PARTY SECOND!

Panel 4: UH, WEED...? — NOT NOW... I'M STUDYING.

Lynn

114

117

YEAH. YOU'RE RIGHT. I GUESS I SHOULD CALL RHETTA.

BONE IDEA.

AFTER ALL, YOU'VE BEEN DATIN' HER FOR OVER 2 YEARS. IT'D BE NICE TO LET HER KNOW YOU'RE GONNA BE GOIN' OUT WITH ANOTHER BABE!

SSST

THAT'S NOT THE WAY IT IS, WEED. WHAT'S HAPPENING BETWEEN DEANNA AN' ME IS A PLATONIC REUNION BETWEEN TWO OLD FRIENDS!

GLUG

BY THE WAY... CAN I BORROW YOUR AFTERSHAVE?

OAT BUDS

MACARONI AND CHEESE

HAND CLEANER

RUT

SOAP

YOU CALLING RHETTA?

YEAH... I GOTTA DO IT SOMETIME, WEED.

I HATE THIS... SHE'S PROBABLY GOING TO CRY. BUT... I NEED SOME FREEDOM ... AND THE ONE THING I PROMISED WAS THAT I'D ALWAYS BE HONEST WITH... HELLO?

IS RHETTA THERE, PLEASE? SURE. UH HUH. UH HUH — OK ... I SEE. WELL, UM... 'BYE.

WHAT IS IT, MIKE? WHERE IS SHE?

OUT... WITH ANOTHER GUY.

I THOUGHT ABOUT YOU SO MANY TIMES LAST SUMMER, DEANNA.

WHEN SCHOOL STARTED, I KNEW YOU WERE IN PHARMACY, SO I'D GO OVER TO THE SCIENCE BUILDINGS OR TO THE HOSPITAL ... HOPING TO SEE YOU WALK BY.

SO THE FACT THAT YOU WERE IN THE STUDENT NEWSPAPER OFFICE AT THE SAME TIME I WAS TODAY, WAS A REAL COINCIDENCE!

OH... NOT REALLY.

131

I THINK WE'LL HAVE TO STOP STUDYING TOGETHER, DEANNA!

WHAT FOR?

.... I KEEP STUDYING THE WRONG THINGS !!

I'D BETTER GO HOME, DEANNA—I HAVE AN' EARLY CLASS TOMORROW.

ME TOO.

HEY, PATTERSON! DEANNA!—WE HEARD YOU TWO WERE A HOT ITEM !!

WELL, IT'S NOT TRUE!

WHAT DO YOU MEAN, IT'S NOT TRUE?!

... IN **THIS** WEATHER ?!!

YOU'RE STILL UP?

YEAH. I'M ON I.V. CAFFEINE' TIL I GET THIS ASSIGNMENT DONE.

SO YOU ACTUALLY TRIED TO COMBINE A DATE WITH STUDYING, RIGHT?

I GOT THROUGH A FULL CHAPTER IN PSYCHOLOGY, WEED, AN' I WENT THROUGH ALL MY HISTORY NOTES.

AN' WHAT DO YOU REMEMBER?

EVERYTHING! I REMEMBER EVERYTHING, OK?

133

135

140